JUN 1 2 1998

CITY PLANNING
IN ANCIENT TIMES

JUN 1 2 1998

The Lerner Archaeology Series

DIGGING UP THE PAST

CITY PLANNING IN ANCIENT TIMES

by Arthur Segal

retold for young readers by Richard L. Currier

 Lerner Publications Company ▪ Minneapolis

ACKNOWLEDGEMENTS

The illustrations are reproduced through the courtesy of: Elsevier P. 6; 12; 19; 22; 25; 28; 53; 54; 57. Studio Vista P. 8; 75. Office du Livre P. 23; 43. Alinari P. 27; 42; 50; 59; 61; 62. Massada P. 33—36; 69—72. Thames and Hudson P. 37; 47; 67. Hunting Aerosurveys Ltd. P. 49. Photocielo, Rome P. 58. Rheinisches Landesmuseum P. 64. After Jon Wilsher P. 65. After W. Stevenson Smith P. 73; 78. Hirmer P. 77. The University of Chicago Press P. 81. After R. Koldewey P. 82.

Designed by Ofra Kamar

LIBRARY OF CONGRESS CATALOGING IN PUBLICATION DATA

Currier, Richard L.
City planning in ancient times.

(Digging up the Past: The Lerner Archaeology Series)
Includes index.
SUMMARY: Examines the art of city planning as it was in ancient times and describes some of the oldest planned cities, now in ruins, of Greece, the Roman Empire, Egypt, and Mesopotamia.

1. Cities and towns — Planning — Juvenile literature. 2. Cities and towns, Ancient — Juvenile literature. [1. Cities and towns — Planning. 2. Cities and towns, Ancient] I. Segal, Arthur. City planning in ancient times. II. Title.

HT166.C86 1977   309.2'62'093   75-5294
ISBN 0-8225-0836-2

International Standard Book Number: 0-8225-0836-2
Library of Congress Catalog Card Number: 75-5294

Manufactured in the United States of America

2   3   4   5   6   7   8   9   10   85   84   83   82   81   80   79

CONTENTS

Timgad, an ancient planned city in North Africa built by the Romans in 100 A.D.

I THE ANCIENT ART OF CITY PLANNING

Introduction

More people live in cities today than at any other time in the history of the human race. Our modern world would be almost unthinkable without the great centers of science, industry, finance, government, art, and learning that are scattered across the earth.

Many of the world's great cities, such as London, Paris, Jerusalem, Moscow, and Peking, were founded thousands of years ago. If you were to walk through the centers of these ancient cities, you would find a maze of narrow, winding streets that twist and turn, cutting across each other at strange angles and in irregular ways. This confusing pattern is an inheritance from the past. In the beginning, many of these cities were small villages that grew haphazardly as people moved in and built houses wherever they could buy land or find room. Later, when the villages began to grow larger and more important, people often made plans for wide,

straight streets and avenues. Thus, the areas away from the center of town were laid out in a regular pattern of streets intersecting each other at right angles to form quarters, squares, and blocks.

Some cities, however, even some very ancient ones, did not grow slowly and gradually from small villages but were deliberately established by a group of people who decided to live in a certain place at a certain time. The founders of these cities and towns often had very definite ideas about just what kind of city they wanted to live in and just how they would build it. This book is about the cities and towns that such people built in the area of the ancient world near the Mediterranean Sea, where the great cultures of ancient Egypt, Greece, and Rome flourished thousands of years ago. We will try to give you some idea of what life was like in those ancient cities. We will also describe some of the many important methods of con-

Overleaf: The Mediterranean world

struction, as well as the special public buildings, that were developed by the ancient city planners.

Although we hear much about city planning in our modern society, it is important to realize that the art of designing a city and building it from scratch is not a modern development like aeronautical engineering or nuclear physics. It is, instead, one of the oldest professional accomplishments of the civilized world.

Why Plan a City?

It is a curious fact that while some of the most important advances in city planning were made by the ancient Greeks and Romans, the cities of Athens and Rome — which were the principal cities of these two great societies — were not planned cities. According to the reports of ancient observers, these famous unplanned cities were almost unbearable to live in. The writer Pausanius, for instance, tells of the poverty seen everywhere in Athens and of the filth that littered the streets of this great center of art, learning, commerce, and science. Ancient Rome, it is said, was so extremely noisy that even the Caesar himself, housed deep within the Imperial Palace, was sometimes disturbed in his sleep! It is difficult to imagine how a city could be so noisy before the invention of cars, planes, buses, trains, motorcycles, bulldozers, jackhammers, pile drivers, and all the other machines that fill our modern cities with their racket. But perhaps you can get some of the flavor of life in that vast, crowded ancient city by reading the words of ancient writers who tried to describe what life was like for the ordinary Roman citizen:

"Do you ask why I often resort to my small fields . . . and the unkempt household of my villa? Neither for thought. . . nor for quiet is there any place in the city for a poor man. School masters in the morning do not let you live; before daybreak, bakers; the hammers of the coppersmiths all day. On this side the money-changer idly rattles on his dirty table Nero's coins, on that the hammerer of Spanish gold-dust beats his well-worn stone with burnished mallet; and Bellona's raving throng [the Roman army] does not rest, . . . nor the blear-eyed huckster of sulphur wares."

"Who but the wealthy get sleep in Rome? . . . The crossing of wagons on the narrow winding streets, the shouts of the herdsmen when brought to a stand, would make sleep impossible for a Prusus or a sea-calf. When the rich man has a call of social duty, the mob makes way for him as he is borne swiftly over their heads in a huge Liburnian car [a type of sedan-chair]... Yet he will arrive before us; hurry as we may, we are blocked by a surging crowd in front, and by a dense mass of people pressing in on us from behind; one man digs an elbow into me, another a hard sedan pole; one bangs a beam, another a wine-cask, against my head. My legs are beplastered with mud; soon huge feet trample on me from every side, and a soldier plants his hobnails firmly on my toe."

In comparision with the uproar that these writers describe, even downtown New York seems almost peaceful! Obviously, the cities of the past were as noisy, dirty, and crowded as modern cities. Ancient builders found that if they could plan cities from the beginning, however, they could avoid some of these problems. By designing cities with wide, straight streets, with parks, fountains, gardens, and squares, and with public buildings such as theaters and gymnasiums, they could make city life far more pleasant.

In recent times, we too have come to realize how important and beneficial intelligent planning can be in the life of a city. Some of our most important modern cities, in fact, were planned from the very start and built in places where no town or city had existed before. Brasilia, the capital of Brazil, is the newest of these planned cities; Washington, D.C. is probably the most important of the planned cities of the modern world.

Modern city planners have a more complex job to do than the ancient planners did, because the modern world, with its advanced technology, is more complex than the ancient world was. But now, as in the past, the city planner must still consider many things: the natural features of the surrounding landscape, a proper division of the city into industrial, residential, and commercial areas, the location of roads, streets, and proper facilities for water, light, air, and the disposal of wastes. All of these things must be taken into account in order to insure the inhabitants of the city a healthier and more comfortable life.

The City Planner's Job

As you read about the ancient planned cities described in these pages, you may notice that they were not all alike. There were many different ways in which a city could be built, and the final design always depended on a combination of several

Overleaf: The Palatine, the most important of the seven hills of Rome, was at the heart of the ancient city.

factors, each one of which influenced the outcome in a different way.

The first factor was the political system of the people who were building the planned city. Were they ruled by a king or despot who made all the decisions himself, or did they live under a more democratic system, in which many different members of the community could participate in decisions about how the city was to be built? Another factor was the reasons people had for building the city in the first place. Was it to be a military center? Then it would have to be well defended, to guard against attack in times of war. Was it to be a center of religious worship? Then land would have to be set aside for the shrines and temples that would be built. Some cities were built as harbors, others to be centers of government. Throughout history, in fact, it has often happened that a new ruler who came to power would decide to build a new capital city. We shall describe one of these new capital cities — built by the last great Pharaoh of ancient Egypt — later in this book.

Another factor that affected the form a city took was the level of technology of the society. The Romans, to give just one example, developed the science and technology of architecture in several important ways, one of which was by learning how to build strong, durable arches that could support structures rising high above the ground. This advance made it possible for them to build great aqueducts — tall, arched structures that carried water from the distant countryside into the heart of the city.

Still another factor affecting a planned city was the wealth of the society. A great and powerful empire could build palaces of magnificent style and splendor, or finance huge public works for the common good. But a group of hopeful colonists or retired soldiers might have little money to invest, and the town they might plan for themselves would have to be modest and simple.

Finally, the site of a planned city influenced its design and form. All the planned cities and towns of the ancient world were built either out in the countryside or at the locations of older settlements. If the new city were built out in the countryside, the natural features of the landscape affected the form of the town itself. In other cases, however, the new city was built at the site of an older city that had been destroyed or simply abandoned. The bricks, stones, and paving of the ruined city might even be used in building the new one, or they might be left to form the foundations of the new settlement. The builders would have to decide whether to build the new city directly on top of the ruins themselves or, as was often the case, to build it near or next to the old city.

The city planners of the past almost never attempted to rebuild an established city unless it had had the misfortune of being destroyed by wars or natural disasters. As long as a city remains standing, the old streets and buildings present a real obstacle to the work of a city planner. When the famous architect Georges Haussmann rebuilt large sections of Paris in the 19th century, for example, he was forced to destroy many lovely ancient buildings in order to achieve his goals. Of course, the elegant avenues and wide boulevards that he designed gave Paris much of the unique character and beauty that it has today. Nevertheless, modern city planners would usually not attempt to make such drastic changes in an established and thriving city. Instead, they build their new cities in unoccupied regions such as Israel's Negev Desert, where there is nothing to interfere with a carefully planned network of streets and a generous distribution of land for residential areas.

The Study of
Ancient City Planning

For a long time, people were unaware of just how much city planning had been done in ancient times. But when archaeologists — scientists who find and study the remains of ancient societies — began to unearth the remains of early civilizations in Europe, Asia, and the Middle East during the last 200 years, they found evidence of ancient planned cities. These scientists discovered that even some of the very oldest cities showed quite clearly, in their straight and regular network of streets and in the careful arrangement of parks and public buildings, that city planners had been at work thousands of years ago, just as they were in the modern world. Another source of information about ancient city planning was found in the writings of a Roman architect named Vitruvius, one of the very few writers of ancient times who paid attention to the work of city planners. The development of aerial photography during World War II also created much interest in ancient city planning. Photographs taken from the air often showed the faint outlines of ancient walls and

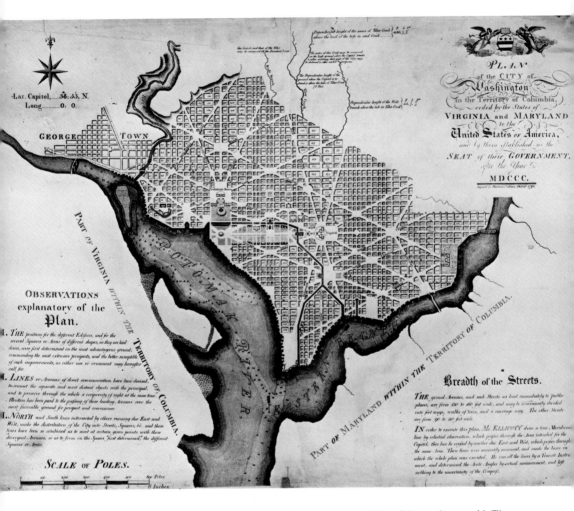

The original plan of Washington, D.C., one of the most famous planned cities of the modern world. The plan was drawn up in the 1790s by Pierre L'Enfant, a French engineer hired by George Washington.

foundations that had never been visible from the ground, and people became aware of how regular and carefully planned some of the ruined cities had once been.

In the following chapters, we will look at some of the oldest planned cities and towns and at the impressive public works and technological achievements of the ancient Romans.

But first we will take a close look at the city planning of ancient Greece, because it was Greek civilization that first introduced the art of city planning to the western world. As you will see, the people of ancient Greece developed many of the characteristics of the city that are still common in the cities we build and live in to this very day.

II THE GREEK CITY

Greece is a small country made up of a mountainous mainland with an irregular, rocky coast and many islands, of all shapes and sizes, scattered across a large part of the Mediterranean Sea. Greek territory stretches from near Italy in the west to the shores of Turkey in the east. The Greek climate is pleasant and warm, but the land is poor; there is little rich farmland and few mineral resources. Ever since ancient times, the Greek people have had to work hard to make even a poor living off their land.

The mountainous Greek countryside and the far-flung Greek islands have always made it difficult for the people of Greece to travel by land from one part of their country to another. This difficulty of transportation and of communication had two important effects on the development of Greek society in ancient times. One effect was to stimulate the use of boats and ships for travel rather than pack animals or wagons.

The Greeks became skilled seafarers and eventually built great fleets of ships for commerce and for war. The other effect was to isolate each region of Greece from the other regions. This isolation made it impossible for a single city or ruler to conquer a huge amount of territory and build a great empire, or even to unify Greece itself under a single government. Throughout ancient times, Greece remained a country of independent city-states, each one of which ruled the surrounding villages and countryside.

Emigrants and Colonizers

Because the citizens of the Greek city-states were individualists with independent spirits and because their land was poor, they soon set out in all directions to find new homes for themselves in other lands. For the most part, the Greek colonists were welcomed wherever they settled because they came peacefully, wishing not to conquer other people but

Right: The rocky coast of Greece

simply to trade with them. The Greek settlers brought with them the much-desired manufactured goods of their civilized society, which the farmers and shepherds of Europe and Asia did not know how to make themselves but were eager to purchase with the hides, lumber, grain, and metals of their own lands.

Greek colonization reached a high point during the seventh and eighth centuries before Christ. During this period of commercial expansion, the Greek cities prospered, growing not only wealthier but also more crowded. This small population explosion touched off a great wave of colonization, and within a short period of time, the seacoasts near Greece were filled with new and bustling Greek towns.

Most of the settlers of the Greek colonies were young and adventurous families from the great Greek cities of Athens, Corinth, and Megara. They had left their homes to begin a new life, just as the pioneers of the American West did not long ago. Because they were adventurous people, they were willing to experiment, to seek new solutions to the urban problems they had left behind in the crowded cities of their homeland.

Although the colonists had left Greece to begin a new life, they brought with them many of the traditions of their Greek heritage. In addition to their speech, their manner of dress, their favorite foods, and their customs, they also brought their democratic traditions. Thus, the land for the new colonies was divided up into equal sections to insure that each family received a fair share of land for its own living quarters. Care was also taken to allow enough space for the erection of the different public buildings that every citizen had a right to use and enjoy. From the beginning, therefore, Greek colonies were planned towns, reflecting the basic political ideas of their inhabitants.

The Greek geographer and historian Deodorus has left us his account of the founding of the Greek colony of Thurioi in southern Italy in 444 B.C. Scholars believe that Thurioi was established in a fashion typical of the founding of most of these new Greek towns.

". . . Having found not far from Sybaris a spring called Thuria, which had a bronze pipe . . . and believing this to be the place where the god had pointed out, they threw a wall about it, and . . . they named it Thurium, after the spring. They divided the city lengthwise by four streets . . . and breadthwise they divided it by three streets. . . .And since the quarters formed by these streets were filled with dwellings, the construction of the city appeared to be good."

Public Life and Public Works

Every Greek town saw itself as an independent state. To maintain its independence, the town was protected by fortifications, so that it could be defended in case of attack. The main fortress of each settlement was called the "acropolis," and it was usually built on the highest ground in or next to the town itself. The famous Greek philosopher Aristotle once remarked that an acropolis was essential only in a town ruled by a few powerful families. In such a town, the acropolis provided a place where the rulers could take shelter if the population rebelled against them. A democratic town, he said, having no need of such a shelter, would not have to build an acropolis. Actually, in many Greek cities, the acropolis served not only as a military stronghold but also as an important center of religious life. The most famous acropolis of all — the acropolis of Athens — was such a religious center. The most important structure built upon it was the Parthenon, a famous temple of the goddess Athena and one of the most revered and beautiful of all the buildings still standing from ancient times.

In addition to the acropolis, sturdy walls were also important features of most Greek towns. Because neighboring independent towns often fought against each other, much attention was devoted to the construction of strong fortress-like walls around the entire town. Such walls were, in fact, standard features of almost all cities and towns throughout the world until modern times. They offered the only means of protecting the inhabitants from foreign armies as well as from the robbers, thieves, pirates, smugglers, and slave-raiders who commonly roamed the countryside.

The walls of the Greek cities were built of stones carefully cut to fit together so well that no cement or mortar was needed. While the streets of the town were straight and crossed each other at right angles, the walls followed an irregular path over the natural contours of the land. Every so often along the length of the wall, stone towers rose three or even four stories in the air. At the top of each tower, there were small windows from which lookouts could

The acropolis of Athens

The 2,000-year-old wall surrounding the Greek city of Eleutherae is still standing today.

search the countryside and defenders of the town could fire upon their enemies, in the event that the town was attacked. Fortified gates provided a passage through the walls and the only means of entrance into the city. When night fell or when the city was under attack, the gates were closed by heavy wooden doors. Towers stood at either side of each gate, to protect this weak spot in the city's defenses.

Perhaps the most important single feature of the ancient Greek city was a large public area called the "agora." In most planned towns and cities, this consisted of a square piece of land paved with stones and bordered on all four sides by several rows of columns. These columns supported a narrow roof that provided a shelter from the burning Mediterranean sun in the summer and from the cold rains that fall throughout the winter months.

The agora was the ancient Greek equivalent of our city hall. The officials of the city met here to conduct the city's business, and the city's archives and public offices were located within it. If statues or monuments honoring the heroes of the town were erected, they were usually placed in the agora for all to see and admire. Although there were usually other areas in the town reserved for marketplaces, the agora itself served as a marketplace as well. The citizens of the town or city would also gather in the agora on important social and religious occasions, and religious rituals honoring the town's gods and heroes were performed there. Since the agora was considered a holy place, certain customs were established to insure that its sanctity was not defiled. A citizen who was accused of murder, for example, was forbidden to enter the agora.

One of the most important of all public places in the ancient Greek city was the theater. The Greeks were enthusiastic dramatists and theatergoers, and the few dozen Greek plays that have survived from ancient times are still considered among the greatest works of literature in the history of civilization. Greek plays were originally performed only twice a year, during religious festivals in honor of Dionysius, the god of wine and fertility. The people of the city would put all their work aside, close up their houses and their shops, and flock to the theater for several days of plays, ceremonies, and merriment. The actors were simply the town's most talented and energetic citizens; almost every family had at least one member performing in the plays, which often had large casts as well as choruses of singers. In some cities, the festivals lasted from dawn to dusk for several days in a row. Going to the theater was like a huge vacation from the dullness and hard work of everyday life.

No Greek city or town was complete without a theater, but it was not the enclosed house-like structure that we use for films, plays, and concerts today. It was a large, open area, usually constructed in the form of a semi-circle and surrounded by rows of seats. The earliest Greek theaters consisted simply of a number of wooden seats arranged around a stage. Later, however, beautiful and expensive theaters were built of stone, usually on the sides of hills or on sloping ground where the contours of the land formed a natural dish-shaped depression. The center of the theater was a flat, round space where the chorus sang and danced; just behind this area was the raised stage, where the actors performed.

Another public building that no Greek city could be without was the gymnasium. The young men of ancient Greece spent many hours

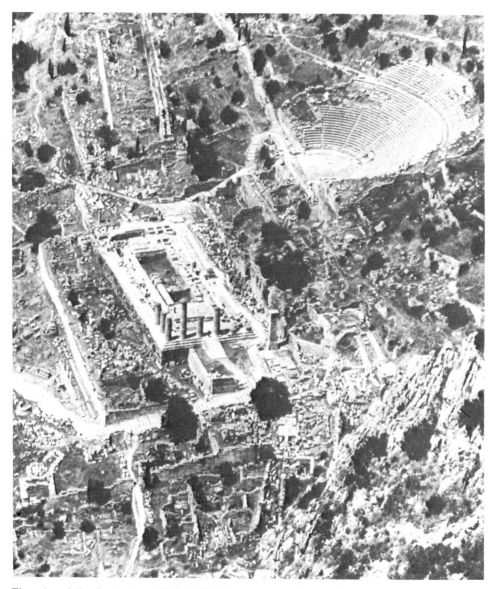

The ruins of the Greek city of Delphi. Delphi's theater can be seen in the upper right corner of the picture.

each day in the gymnasium, learning to develop and control their bodies while at the same time cultivating their mental abilities through the study of poetry, philosophy, and music. In the early days of ancient Greece, the typical gymnasium was nothing more than a large, open field surrounded by trees and a fence. As time passed and Greek society grew more prosperous and refined, the gymnasium gradually developed into a large, complex structure built around the sides of an open courtyard. In the major cities some gymnasiums had bathhouses and enclosed halls, in which the men trained even during the cold winter months.

In addition to these structures, many Greek cities had a stadium as well. This was a long, narrow racing track, rounded at one end and straight at the other. Along both of the long sides and behind the rounded end, there were rows of seats for spectators, as in the Greek theaters. The most famous of all the ancient stadiums was built at the town of Olympia, where the Olympic games were held in ancient times. This immense stadium held up to 45,000 spectators, making it as large as many of our own football stadiums. In the ruins of some of these ancient Greek stadiums, many of the original stone seats can still be seen.

Private Life and Private Houses

The Greeks enjoy such a beautiful climate and have such a strong appreciation of public life that to this day they spend little time at home, preferring instead to gather in squares and marketplaces, cafes and coffee houses, where they eat, argue, sing, dance, gossip, and carry on their many occupations. The Greeks of ancient times must have differed little in this respect from their modern descendants. We know this because most of the houses found in the ruins of even the rich and powerful Greek cities are poor and modest in appearance, compared with the luxury and magnificence of their public buildings.

The entrance to the ordinary house of those times opened into a corridor that led to a small central courtyard. On one side of the courtyard, there were bathrooms and a kitchen. On another side were the rooms where the family slept, ate, and stored their valuable possessions. A kind of parlor where guests were received was located on one side of the entrance corridor, while on the other side there was a workroom that opened onto the street.

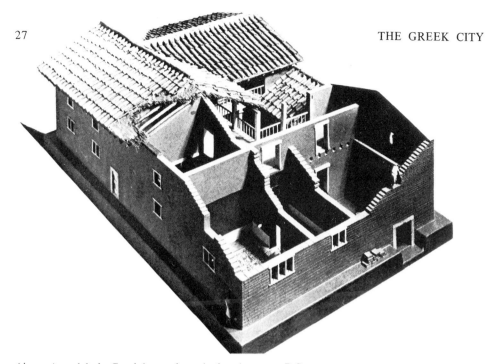

Above: A model of a Greek house, from the fourth century B.C.
Overleaf: The stadium of Athens was reconstructed for the first modern Olympic games, held in 1896.

These houses were built of bricks and had stone foundations. Their roofs were made of wooden beams and were covered with tiles. Most of the activity in the house took place in and around the central courtyard, and most of the doors and windows opened not onto the street but onto the courtyard itself. On the outside, there was only a door or two, and perhaps several small windows. Houses like this are typical of many Mediterranean countries to this very day. You can also see them by the hundreds of thousands in the rural areas of Mexico, where people still follow the traditions that the Spanish *conquistadores* brought with them from the Mediterranean centuries ago.

In a later period of Greek history, some of the houses in the Greek cities became less modest in appearance. During these years, the power and influence of Greek-speaking people spread throughout much of the ancient world, and the Greek cities became less concerned with the rights of individual citizens. They were also less interested in maintaining the democratic philosophy and the public spirit that had been the

source of Greek greatness in earlier times. While public life declined, some of the wealthy and important Greeks built themselves beautiful and luxurious homes, spacious and richly decorated. The central courtyards of these houses were decorated with mosaics and surrounded by columns. In the center of the courtyard there were altars dedicated to the various gods that were believed to protect the house. On one side of the courtyard, there was a pool of rainwater. The most important room in these luxurious houses was called the "prostas"; in this room a fire was always kept burning, and it was here that the daily life of the household centered. On either side of the prostas were rooms where the women and children of the household lived, and behind it was a garden.

While the houses that most of us live in today are quite different from the houses of the ancient Greeks, many people who live in warm climates have homes very much like these ancient dwellings. And although our cities lack some of the important features of the ancient Greek city or town, our own lives would hardly be the same without the town halls, stadiums, and theaters that we inherited from the Greeks.

III SOME PLANNED CITIES OF ANCIENT GREECE

The Rebuilding of Miletus

One of the most famous Greek cities of ancient times was the settlement of Miletus, located in Asia Minor in an area that is now part of the nation of Turkey. Miletus had grown up in haphazard fashion, with the narrow, winding streets that were typical of that region. The city was well known to all Greeks, because it was one of the earliest centers of Greek science and philosophy. Centuries before Athens achieved greatness in learning, Miletus was the home of some of the greatest masters of mathematics, geometry, astronomy, and philosophy.

During the sixth century before Christ, the cities and towns of Asia Minor fell under the rule of the Persians, who built a vast empire across the lands of the Middle East. Proud of their independence and unhappy under foreign rule, the conquered Greek settlers of Asia Minor united under the leadership of the people of Miletus and rebelled against the Persians. For this act of defiance, the Persians retaliated, and in 494 B.C. the Persian army completely destroyed Miletus, killing or capturing many of its citizens.

The destruction of Miletus was the cause of great horror and bitterness throughout all of Greece. The Greek historian Herodotus tells us that when a play about the conquest of Miletus was performed, the Greek audience burst into tears of grief. The unlucky playwright was rebuked for having caused the audience suffering and was forbidden ever to stage the play again.

Even after the destruction of Miletus, the conflict between the Greeks and the Persians was far from over. For 15 years, periods of peace alternated with periods of war, during which the Persians captured Athens and many other Greek cities before being driven back. Finally, in the year 479 B.C., the Greeks won a decisive victory against the Persian army, and the Persians withdrew from Greece completely. The surviving citizens of Miletus returned to the ruins of their city to build again.

The rebuilding of Miletus was the occasion for great joy throughout Greece. A young architect named Hippodamus — who had been born in Miletus before the wars with Persia — was partly responsible for planning the new city. According to Aristotle, it was Hippodamus who invented the city plan that divided the settlement into quarters by using streets that intersected at right angles. The exact role Hippodamus played in rebuilding Miletus is unknown, but we do know that shortly after Miletus was recreated as a planned town, Hippodamus was invited to come to Athens itself. There he was given the extremely important job of planning the port of Piraeus, Athens' sister city and principal harbor. To this day, if you arrive in Athens by sea, you must first dock in the deep and well-protected harbor of Piraeus.

Although the ancient Greeks believed that Hippodamus *invented* city planning, modern scholars disagree. They think it is more likely that he simply refined the knowledge of city planning that existed in Asia Minor at that time, bringing it to the Greek mainland and successfully applying it to the important task of planning the new harbor. Whatever the actual facts may have been, however, one thing is certain. Before Hippodamus' lifetime, city planning was virtually unknown in Greece, but by the time he died, the planning of cities with regular streets had become something of a passion with the ancient Greeks.

Paestum, Miletus, and Olynthus

While Miletus eventually became the most important and influential of the planned cities in Greece, it was not the oldest community that had been deliberately planned and established by Greek citizens. This distinction belongs to a small Greek colony called Paestum, located on the southwestern coast of Italy.

Right: A medieval city in Italy with winding, irregular streets

Overleaf left: With its tall buildings and straight streets, New York City is an extreme example of a modern urban center.

Overleaf right: A triumphal arch symbolizing Rome's military victories over its enemies

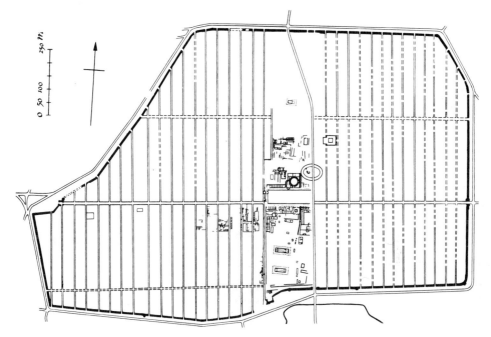

Above: A diagram of the city plan of Paestum

Left: Wealthy Romans decorated their homes with frescoes such as this one depicting a mythological scene.

Paestum was founded in the year 524 B.C., fully 45 years before the rebuilding of Miletus. The colony flourished in its early years, but eventually, it lost its independence as a Greek city-state when the Romans extended the borders of their growing republic into the region of southern Italy.

Paestum was surrounded by a wall that today remains complete throughout its entire length, even though it was first built 2,500 years ago. The area of the town itself was divided by streets into a network of perfect squares. The highway upon which Paestum was built ran straight through the town, entering through the east gate of the city wall and leaving through the west gate. The center of Paestum was set aside for public buildings. The remains of a market, a theater, and a city hall are still visible among the ruins, but these appear to have been built long after Paestum was founded and may not have been part of the original city plan. The remains of three temples have also survived, however, and they seem to have been part of the original plan of this oldest of Greek planned towns.

When Miletus was rebuilt as a planned town, it turned out to be one of the most beautiful and well-formed of the Greek communities. No doubt this is one important reason why Miletus became the model for dozens of new settlements that were founded in Greece over the following two centuries. Miletus was built on a peninsula of land about one and one-quarter miles (2 kilometers) long. The only hill on the peninsula rose up between two small inlets that were used as the city's harbors. There were three residential areas in Miletus, and in each area a network of streets divided the land into small squares within which private homes were built, one alongside the other.

The center of the city, where the three living areas joined each other, was designed to be the civic center of Miletus. There were two small agoras that served as marketplaces, and a huge central agora connected to them, which was the very heart of the city. This enormous agora covered an area equal to that of *four* football fields! On the ground above each of the harbors stood a temple and, next to one of these temples, the gymnasium. Finally, the theater was built on the slopes of the only hill, giving it an impressive view of the harbor. Looking at Miletus from above, we can understand why it inspired the Greeks of Athens to embark on an ambitious project of city planning. This city was not only designed to be functional and efficient; it was also designed to be beautiful.

Olynthus was another Greek town that was destroyed during the wars with Persia. When it was rebuilt many years afterwards, the citizens chose a new town site, close to the site of the old town. The new Olynthus was designed with five main streets running north and south and a large number of smaller, narrow streets that crossed the main streets at right angles. The center of government and public life was established, not at the center of Olynthus, but on the southwestern side, at one end of the town's widest street.

Most of the houses found in the ruins of Olynthus are nearly identical in size and construction. This evi-

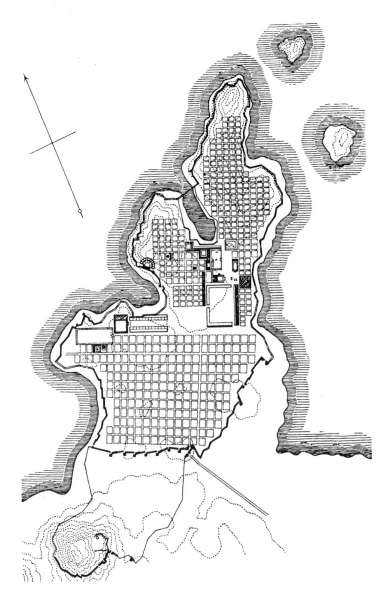

The plan of Miletus, a Greek city rebuilt in 479 B.C.

dence suggests that the citizens of the community put into practice some of the ideals of equality for which the Greeks had become so widely known. The sections of land set aside for each house were all equal in size, and all the main streets and all the cross streets were exactly the same width, except for the street that led to the civic center. The plan of Olynthus is so even and regular, in fact, that archaeologists have often expressed amazement that a community designed and built 2,500 years ago could look so much like a modern town.

The Cities of Alexander the Great and His Successors

Throughout most of the fifth century B.C., the Greeks were either fighting with the Persians or squabbling among themselves. During this long period of conflict, the Greeks' desire to establish new colonies and expand into other lands had diminished considerably. But the rise of a bold and ambitious leader named Alexander during the fourth century marked the beginning of a new period of Greek expansion.

Unlike the Greeks of an earlier period, who had left their homeland to promote trade and commerce, the Greeks under Alexander embarked upon a program of military conquests. Alexander was a brilliant military leader, and within a few short years he had not only established himself as the most powerful ruler in Greece but had also conquered the entire Persian Empire, establishing control over the lands east of Greece as far as the borders of India!

Alexander the Great — as he came to be called — was a sincere admirer of the rich and powerful societies of the East. He dreamed of a great empire in which the industriousness and scientific knowledge of Greece could combine with the wealth and splendor of the East. Alexander envisioned an ideal state in which Greeks and Persians would live together in harmony, and he encouraged Greeks to settle in the newly conquered Persian lands.

Thus there arose a new wave of Greek migration and colonization, but this time the techniques and advantages of city planning were known and accepted throughout Greece. All along the route of Alexander's conquests, dozens of planned towns were built. The Greek soldiers who followed and fought with Alexander settled in these towns, married Persian women, and formed the first communities in which the Greek and

Persian cultures were meant to blend, creating the basis for the new society Alexander dreamed of.

In the midst of consolidating his newly won empire, however, Alexander fell ill and died, at the age of 33. Without the genius of Alexander's leadership, the new empire quickly fell apart. Many of the settlements were deserted and fell into ruins, and some of the conquered lands broke free of the Greek influence that had arrived with Alexander. But other settlements blossomed into strong and prosperous cities, proudly displaying the Greek flag.

Alexander and Dinocrates

Certainly one of the most unusual aspects of Alexander's career was the fact that he was accompanied on his conquests by an architect named Dinocrates, whose job was to plan the new cities and towns that Alexander established throughout the lands he conquered. The Roman writer Vitruvius, whom we mentioned earlier as one of the few sources of written information about city planning in the ancient world, tells an interesting story about how Alexander's association with Dinocrates began.

Dinocrates was young and ambi-tious himself, and like many Greek men of his time, he wanted to join Alexander's forces and participate in the exciting and profitable campaign of conquest upon which Alexander had embarked. But Alexander — who was king of Macedonia, in addition to being a successful conqueror — was constantly surrounded by his servants and advisors, and Dinocrates despaired of ever getting close enough to talk to him.

Finally, Dinocrates decided to act boldly, in the hope of getting Alexander's attention. He removed his clothes and dressed himself in a lion skin, the traditional costume of the mythical hero Hercules. When he saw his opportunity, he leaped in front of Alexander, declaring in a loud voice that he wanted to accompany the conqueror on his military campaigns, acting as the architect and city-planner of the new towns that were to be established. Amused by Dinocrates' strange appearance, and perhaps impressed by his boldness, Alexander stopped to talk to him and listen to his ideas about the planning of towns and cities. As a result of this conversation, Alexander agreed to take Dinocrates with him on all his future campaigns and to give him the important job of planning the new settlements of Alexander's empire. It would be impossible to describe even half of these numerous cities and towns, which are scattered over the entire Middle East, so instead we will tell you about two of the most interesting examples of Dinocrates' work.

Priene and Alexandria

The town of Priene was built high above the River Meander in Asia Minor, on a steep and rocky mountainside. Because of its breathtaking view, Priene was considered one of the most beautiful and picturesque towns of the ancient world. Priene was surrounded by a wall about a mile and half (two and a half kilometers) long, and the town's acropolis was built on the very top of the mountain. Just below the acropolis stood a temple, and beneath that, the theater. The agora was down in the center of the town, and the stadium and gymnasium were built just below it. These public buildings were among the most beautiful in Greece; the huge agora, standing on the hill-

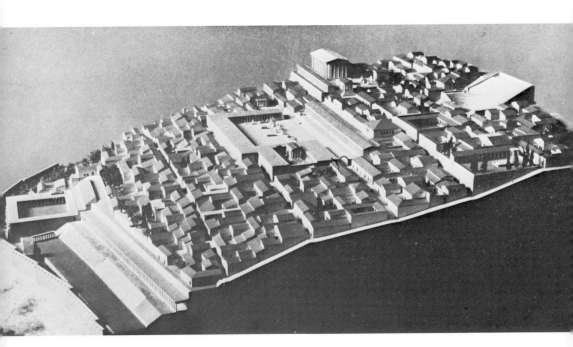

A model of Priene

The meeting place of the city council of Priene

side and flanked on either side by a temple, must have been an especially impressive and beautiful sight. Despite the steep slope of the mountainside, the streets of Priene were still built according to the ideal, with parallel streets crossing each other at right angles. Some of the streets, however, ran straight up the mountainside, so instead of ordinary paving the builders had to install flights of steps.

Of all the cities established by Alexander and planned by Dinocrates, the most important and successful was the city in Egypt that still bears the conqueror's name: Alexandria. Egypt had always been one of the most important societies of the ancient world, and when Alexander dreamed of a great world empire, he naturally founded a settlement in Egypt. Alexandria was built on the shores of the Mediterranean, just west of the delta region where the Nile River enters the sea.

Alexandria soon developed into one of the most important centers of philosophy, poetry, and the arts in the ancient world. The lighthouse of Alexandria was considered one of the Seven Wonders of the Ancient World, and the library of the city was one of the largest and most important of its time.

Tens of thousands of manuscripts — all laboriously written or copied by hand — filled the rooms of this great library, and scholars came from many other countries to make use of its scientific and intellectual riches. One of the most tragic events of ancient times was the destruction of the library at Alexandria. This event occurred near the beginning of the Christian era, when the soldiers of the Roman ruler Julius Caesar, who were fighting to aid the Egyptian queen Cleopatra, burned this great library to the ground.

At that moment in history, an important change was taking place in the ancient world, as the power and influence of the Greeks gradually gave way to the growing power of the Romans. As Roman society grew, prospered, and expanded, it grew more civilized and sophisticated. After the Romans had established their military power in the eastern Mediterranean, they strove to learn the arts and sciences of civilization from the Greeks, whom they sincerely admired. City planning was only one of the arts and sciences that the Romans took from Greek culture, of course, but it is the one that concerns *us* the most.

An aerial view of Dura-Europos, a city in Syria established around 300 B.C. by a successor of Alexander the Great

IV CITIES OF THE ROMAN EMPIRE

The Etruscans

The great culture of ancient Rome drew its strength and wisdom from two important sources. One source was the civilization of the ancient Greeks, who established many colonies in the south of Italy and whom the Romans admired for their artistic, cultural, and scientific achievements. The other source of Roman culture was the civilization of the Etruscans, a people who inhabited the northern part of the Italian peninsula, living in a loose federation of independent cities and towns.

The Etruscans were skilled metalworkers, especially accomplished in the forging of iron, but they also excelled in the production of ceramic wares, such as bricks, tiles, and pottery.

From our point of view, however, the Etruscans' most important skill was in the field of architecture. Among the many techniques that Roman architects learned from the Etruscans was the art of building round or conical vaults of brick or stone, which the Etruscans used in constructing their burial mounds.

Etruscan society experienced its period of greatest prosperity and expansion during the sixth and seventh centuries B.C., at about the same time that the Greeks were founding colonies along the shores of the Mediterranean and the Black Sea. Compared to most of the civilized peoples of the ancient world, however, the Etruscans were rather rude and barbaric, and they never achieved the degree of refinement enjoyed by the Egyptians, Greeks, Romans, and others. After the sixth century B.C., Etruscan society declined and Roman society grew in power and importance. Eventually, Roman civilization seemed to swallow up the neighboring Etruscans, and their language and culture disappeared. The Etruscans' architectural techniques lived on, however, forming a basis for later Roman achievements.

Right: The Romans were very skillful in the use of brick, which was their favorite building material.

Roman Architects
and City Planners

The Greeks loved to build their houses, temples, and other public buildings out of stone, even though it took much time and labor to chisel each stone to the correct shape and fit it into the structure in a way that was permanent and secure. The Romans, on the other hand, preferred to use bricks and mortar, because these materials were lighter and easier to handle, and because they could be mass-produced quickly. Another advantage of bricks was that they were cheap to make. Moreover, the raw materials for bricks and mortar were — unlike stone — plentiful throughout the Roman countryside, thus making it unnecessary to transport building materials over long distances at the cost of further time and money. Perhaps the most important advantage of using bricks and mortar was that of speed. The Romans wanted to build and expand their cities rapidly, and large structures could be built quickly out of bricks and mortar, in contrast to the great patience required when building with stone.

Though the Romans built most of their structures out of brick, they continued to appreciate the beauty of stone. For this reason, the Romans often covered the walls of their brick buildings with smooth slabs of marble, so that they would look as beautiful as their Greek counterparts.

In some respects, the Romans surpassed the Greeks in architectural achievements. They developed the technique of building arches and vaults to a high art, making it possible to enclose large spaces without having to fill the spaces with columns to keep the roof from falling in. Using these skills of engineering and design, the Romans built huge stadiums, marketplaces, aqueducts, and even apartment buildings, some of which were as much as five stories high!

The Romans displayed the same practical nature and love of size and speed when they began to build colonies in other lands. Roman colonies were often military in origin. The government sent veteran soldiers of the Roman army to settle in military towns in order to protect the interests of the Roman state and defend the conquered territories from attack or rebellion. Thus, the Roman settlers did not really come voluntarily to begin a new life, like the early Greek colonists. Partly for this reason, the Romans were interested in building the new settlements as

Above: Roman roads were noted for their excellent engineering. This photograph shows an old Roman road cutting through the agricultural land of modern Italy.

Overleaf: A model of a five-story Roman building with shops on the ground floor and apartments on the upper levels

rapidly, cheaply, and efficiently as possible. The most important consideration was the strategic or military value of a particular location or city plan. After that, the city planners would consider the quality of the nearby farmland, the availability of water, and other factors that would affect the standard of living of the inhabitants. The beauty or esthetic value of the planned settlement, if it was considered at all, came last.

Not all the planned towns were established for military purposes, however. The city of Ostia, on the west coast of Italy, was built to serve as the seaport of Rome, just as

Piraeus was built to serve as the seaport of Athens. And one Roman emperor founded a town in Egypt for sentimental reasons. This town, called "Antinoupolis," was established in memory of the emperor's friend Antinous, who drowned in the Nile.

The Standard Plan
for a Roman Town

The Romans were an organized, efficient, and industrious people, and this was, no doubt, one of the secrets of their immense success in founding the largest, most secure, and most prosperous empire the world has ever known. Since the Romans built colonies at an extremely rapid rate, they devised a standard plan for their colonial towns, so that each town would not have to be designed from scratch.

The Roman colony was either square or rectangular in shape. One main road ran through the colony from east to west, and another main road ran through from north to south. The place where these two roads intersected would be the center of town. Once they had marked out the town boundaries and had established the location of these two main streets, the rest of the area was quickly filled in. As you probably

have guessed, the remaining area of the town was filled with streets that ran parallel to the two main roads. These streets intersected at right angles to form a number of regular-shaped blocks, which the Romans called "islands," perhaps because they were separated from each other by the intersecting streets. Finally, the entire town was enclosed by strong walls, and the two main roads passed through four gates, one in each of the four walls, to continue out into the countryside.

The founding of a new city or town had great religious significance for the ancient Romans, and certain ceremonies were faithfully performed whenever a new settlement was established. First, one of the founders would say the necessary prayers and perform the correct rituals to insure that the gods of the region were not offended by the establishment of the new settlement in their midst. Then the all-important ritual of plowing the town's borders was performed.

Using a team of oxen, one man would plough a single furrow in the earth where one of the town walls was to be built. Then he would turn and plow another furrow at right angles to the first one. Turning again at each of the corners of the town's

A drawing of a typical Roman temple. The platform, or podium, forms the base of the structure.

borders, he would eventually reach the spot where he had begun, having plowed a square or rectangular shape in the earth.

Ancient people believed that their gods were willing to protect and defend their cities and towns as long as the proper altars were erected in their honor, and as long as the townspeople observed the correct religious ceremonies. After the borders of the town were plowed, it was believed that the gods of the town would be willing to defend only the land inside the plow lines.

Thus, the settlers were careful to build the entire town within these borders.

In every Roman town, a temple was built on the highest point of land to honor the three gods of the Roman Capitol: Jupiter, Juno and Minerva. This temple was called the "Capitolium," and it was the most sacred place in the town. If the town was constructed on completely flat ground, then the Capitolium would be built upon a special platform, to raise it above the level of the surrounding streets and houses.

A stone sculpture showing a Roman crane (left) in action. The power that runs the crane is supplied by human workers (lower left).

The architect and writer Vitruvius, explaining the correct way to plan the location of the various shrines and temples that the inhabitants of a new town might decide to erect, had some interesting comments to make. After stating that the Capitolium was to be built on the highest ground, he goes on to describe the proper location of buildings erected to honor other gods. According to Vitruvius, a temple in honor of Mercury, the god of trade and travel, should be built in the forum (the civic center of the town, similar to the Greek agora). Shrines in honor of Isis and Serapis (Egyptian gods of fertility and of the underworld) were to be erected in the business quarter. A shrine dedicated to Apollo (the god of the sun, prophesy, medicine, and poetry) or to Bacchus (the god of wine) was to be located next to the theater; a shrine to Hercules (a hero of extraordinary size and strength), at the gymnasium or the circus; and to Mars (the god of war), in the parade ground outside the walls of the city. In addition to the shrine of Mars, Vitruvius writes that the shrine of Venus (the goddess of love and sex) was also to be built outside the walls of the city, "so that venereal pleasure may not be customary to young men and women in the city."

The Public Buildings and Their Use

While the Roman planned towns may not always have been as beautiful as many of the Greek planned towns, the Romans' great technical skill and engineering abilities provided certain comforts of life that few other ancient communities enjoyed. The streets of Roman towns were wide and straight, and they were often paved. There was a constant supply of pure water, brought to the town by aqueducts that often carried it from distant sources. Most Roman towns had bathhouses and sewage systems that made possible a degree of cleanliness and sanitation simply unheard of in most parts of the world at that time. The cities of northern and western Europe, for example, did not achieve a similar level of public sanitation until modern times.

Every Roman town provided its citizens with a rich and exciting cultural life. Most towns had a theater for plays, an amphitheater for athletic games, and a hippodrome for horse races. The wealthy citizens of the town were expected to pay for these entertainments out of their own pockets. In the city of Rome, the responsibility for providing these plays, games, races, and circuses fell upon the shoulders of the emperor himself. When the Emperor Tiberius, who was known as something of a miser, cut the budget for the public games, the citizens of Rome were angered almost to the point of violence.

The theaters and amphitheaters were generally the largest and most beautiful public buildings of the Roman cities and towns. The famous Roman Colosseum, largest of all the ancient amphitheaters, held 45,000 people and was honeycombed with an intricate network of stables, passageways, dressing rooms, and storerooms. After 2,000 years of sun, rain, and wind, the Colosseum is still largely intact, although in the last 50 years it has begun to crumble. The ancient building has become a victim of the constant stream of cars, trucks, and buses that flow around it on the busy Roman streets, shaking the ground beneath this monumental ruin and, in so doing, shaking it apart.

The public life of all ancient Roman communities centered around a place called the "forum." This was an open area, usually surrounded by an arched portico or a series of columns that provided some protection against the weather. Next to the forum was an enclosed structure called the "basilica," which served as a market and as a place for public business during the cold and rainy months of winter.

Close to the forum was the public bathhouse, one of the real luxuries of Roman society, and certainly one of the most distinctive features of the Roman life-style. One section of the bathhouse was reserved exclusively for men, and the other was reserved exclusively for women. Needless to say, the men got the larger share. Each section was further divided into various rooms, which had pools of water of three different temperatures: cold, lukewarm, and hot. Some of the more luxurious bathhouses in the larger towns and cities had other sections and rooms as well, where the inhabitants could get a massage, do physical exercises, or simply mingle with the other bathers. The Roman bathhouse was an important place for social gatherings, and it was used in much the same way as the social clubs of the modern world are used today.

One last Roman structure deserves mention, even though it is not really a building. This is the triumphal arch. The Romans had perfected the

Right: An artist's conception of the interior of the Baths of Caracalla, the most luxurious bathhouse in ancient Rome

The ruins of the forum at Pompeii. The forum was the center of activity in all Roman towns.

The basilica at Pompeii, where public business was conducted during bad weather

technique of building high and graceful arches out of bricks and mortar, and they used them not only for building theaters, aqueducts, and bridges, but for constructing monuments as well. An arch would be erected to honor some famous and important person – perhaps the emperor who ruled at that time – or to commemorate some important event – such as a military victory. Many of the enormous triumphal arches built in Rome are still standing today, adorned with elaborate sculptures and inscriptions that explain or depict the purposes for which they were built.

The Romans' Brand of City Planning

As in so many other areas of civilized life, the Romans borrowed much of what they knew of city planning from the Greeks before them. But Roman city planning was not just a copy of the achievements of the Greeks; everything the Romans did expressed their own special style and character. While the Greek planned town was designed to reflect a political ideal or an appreciation of the beauty of art and nature, the Roman cities reflected a concern with the practical side of life.

The Romans built their planned towns quickly, efficiently, and cheaply. Nevertheless, much technical skill, as well as thought and concern for the welfare of the inhabitants, went into the design and construction of the Roman planned city or town.

Some Roman settlements were destroyed or abandoned when, after several centuries, Roman civilization declined and disintegrated, but many others lived on as independent centers of civilized life, to become some of the famous capital cities of modern Europe. London, Vienna, Paris, and Turin all began as Roman colonies, and of course Rome itself has remained one of the world's most important cities, from ancient times to the present.

Above: Triumphal arches such as these were scattered throughout the Roman Empire.

Overleaf: The aqueduct of Claudius, which brought water into the imperial city of Rome.

An aerial photograph of Trier, Germany, a city established by the Romans almost 2,000 years ago

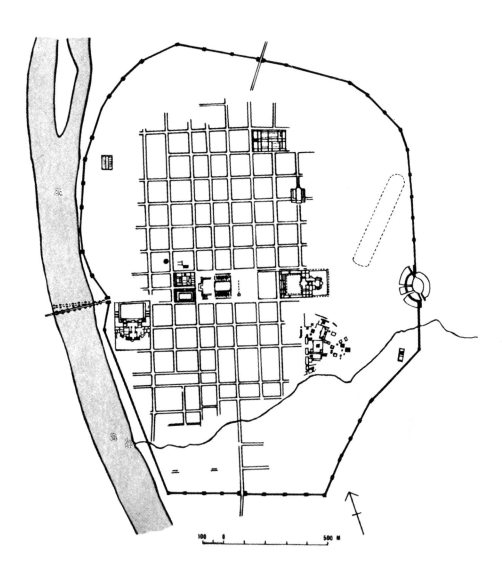

This drawing of the original Roman plan of Trier shows clearly how the modern city still follows the ancient pattern.

V EGYPT AND MESOPOTAMIA

Egypt and Mesopotamia were the cradles of civilization in the western world. All the civilized societies that arose and flourished in Europe, the Mediterranean, and the Middle East were offshoots of one or the other of these extremely ancient civilizations. The first cities sprang up in Egypt and Mesopotamia thousands of years before ancient Greece or Rome even existed, and the ruins of ancient Egypt filled the Greeks and Romans with the same awe and wonder that their own ruins now inspire in us.

Both of these civilizations made great advances in astronomy, mathematics, architecture, metallurgy, writing, and warfare during the two or three thousand years before the birth of Christ. Both arose in great river valleys, where farmland was rich and fertile, where the climate was warm, and where the river waters could be channeled into ditches and canals to irrigate the fields. All of these factors contributed to the development of these two first and oldest civilizations.

The Egyptians

The inhabited area of Egypt is a long, narrow strip of land on both sides of the Nile River, surrounded by thousands of square miles of barren desert. The Nile arises in the mountains of East Africa, and it runs northward through the Sahara Desert until it empties into the Mediterranean Sea. Every year during the month of June, the waters of the Nile begin to rise, overflowing the river banks in July and August and depositing a rich layer of fresh mud on the soil. This renewal of the fertility of the land each year assures the inhabitants of the Nile Valley of a dependable agricultural system.

From the very beginning, the ancient Egyptians learned how to build dams and water channels to control the flow of water at different times of year, so as to insure a plentiful harvest. But it is easy to see how the necessity of controlling the Nile's waters might have become a source of conflict among the inhabitants of

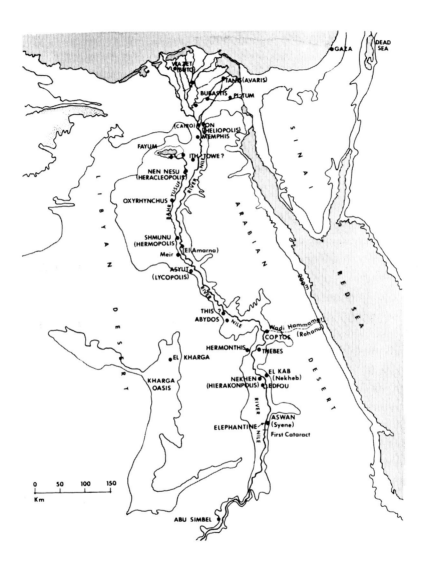

The land of the Egyptians

Egypt. Neighboring farmers might have been inclined to disagree about who should get the irrigation water, when it should be turned on and off, where the dams and channels should be built, and so on.

Most archaeologists and historians believe that the Egyptians established cities and central governments as early as they did because they needed some central authority to control the irrigation projects upon which their wealth and survival depended. Whatever the precise reason, the Egyptians did create a strong central government headed by a Pharaoh, a government able to build and control public works on a large scale, including the planning and construction of towns and cities.

In contrast to the restless and warlike societies all around them, the Egyptians were always a fairly quiet and industrious people. They developed a system of writing with pictures, called "hieroglyphics," which they used to record hundreds of thousands of events, and these writings are the source of much of what we know about these remarkable people. The tombs and pyramids that they built in honor of their dead Pharaohs are also convincing evidence of their great ability and industry. The Egyptians' experience in designing and constructing not only large public works (such as irrigation projects) but also immense public monuments (such as the tombs and pyramids) gave them the skills and experience to plan and construct their own settlements, long before the Greeks and Romans appeared on the scene.

Right: The Parthenon, a beautiful temple on the acropolis of Athens, was dedicated to the goddess Athena.

Overleaf left: The Romans carried their style of architecture even to the distant city of Petra, located in present-day Jordan. This tomb cut out of rock is carved in the shape of a Roman temple.

Overleaf right: Although partially destroyed, the 2,000-year-old Fabricius Bridge still stands in Rome today.

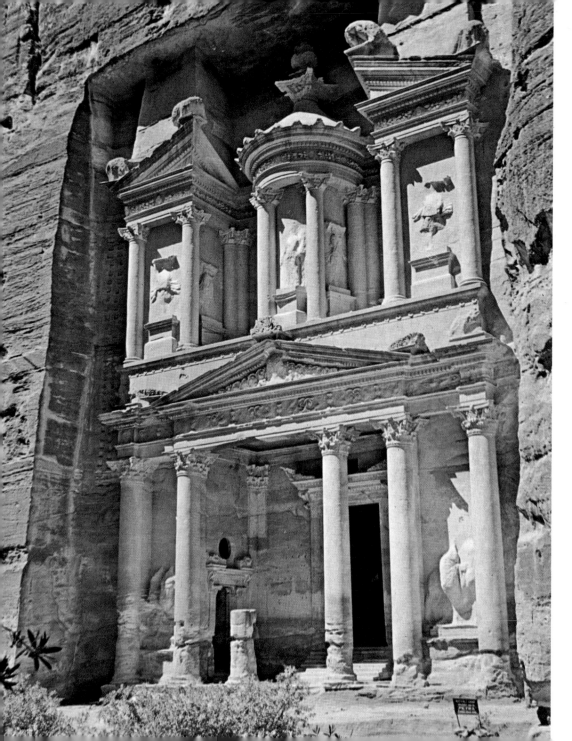

Soldiers, Dreamers, and Pyramid-Builders

The Nile River Valley becomes more arid and more sparsely populated as one travels south, toward the river's source. In ancient times this barren region along the upper Nile was called "Nubia." The Pharaohs went to great pains to protect Nubia from the tribes living in the surrounding deserts, because valuable mines were located there and because it was the gateway to the peaceful farms and villages downriver. For these reasons, the Egyptians built a number of military settlements in Nubia.

These settlements represent some of the oldest planned towns in the ancient world. They were enclosed by thick walls and designed with a bareness and efficiency that is typical of military bases all over the world. The area inside the town walls

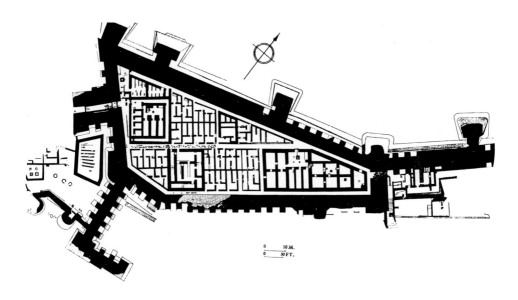

Above: The plan of Urunarti, an early Egyptian fortress town located on the upper Nile

Left: An ancient Roman aqueduct near Nimes, France. The lower level of the aqueduct serves as a road bridge over the Gard River.

was divided into quarters, each with its own function. One quarter was reserved for storerooms, another for living quarters, the third for a temple, and the last for a fortress. Even the small area inside the fortress itself was divided by a small network of planned and patterned streets.

In addition to establishing military settlements in Nubia, the Egyptians built planned towns in other parts of their kingdom. One of these was a town named Kahun. When archaeologists excavated the site of this ancient settlement, they hoped to settle an old question. Kahun was a planned town established for the purpose of providing a home for the workers who built one of the ancient pyramids. Scholars and historians had long wondered just how many people were needed to build a pyramid. While most of the experts agreed that hundreds of thousands of workers must have been employed on these colossal projects, there was no way of determining an exact figure. Scientists hoped that by studying the houses of the laborers' town, and by counting the number of houses, they could determine the figure with greater accuracy.

To everyone's surprise, the town of Kahun turned out to have enough houses for only a few thousand workers, a far lower number than anyone supposed. The old theories — according to which hundreds of thousands of slaves labored under terrible conditions to build the pyramids — were, to some extent, disproved. The workers' houses, while not luxurious, were still spacious and comfortable, each consisting of a small central courtyard surrounded by two or three bedrooms and a small storeroom.

At one end of the town there was a group of luxurious buildings, quite different in size and appearance from the workers' modest houses. Each of these houses was built around a large courtyard bordered on one side by a row of columns. Living rooms were arranged around the courtyard, and the bedrooms contained raised platforms for the beds. These houses, which even had guest rooms and bathrooms, doubtless belonged to the engineers and foremen who supervised the work of constructing the pyramid. Once the pyramid was completed, Kahun was abandonded, and the town was soon buried in the drifting desert sands.

The most interesting and spectacular planned city of ancient Egypt is called "Amarna." It was the capital of a young and idealistic Pharaoh

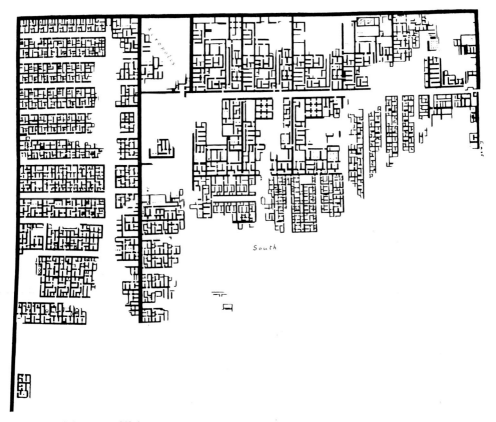

The plan of the town of Kahun

named Akhenaton, a revolutionary figure in Egyptian history. While the Pharaohs before him had observed the worship of many gods and had supported the tremendous inequalities between rich and poor that existed in Egypt, Akhenaton dreamed of a new and more democratic society, with all people, rich and poor, united in the worship of a single god. During his reign, Akhenaton abolished the worship of the old gods and announced that henceforth everyone would worship only the sun-god, Aton. Before long, the young Pharaoh decided to leave the old royal capital at Thebes and build a new and better capital farther up the Nile, a city dedicated to the worship of Aton.

Amarna, as this capital is known to us today, was built on the east bank of the Nile, about 250 miles (400 kilometers) up the river from Thebes. The town itself was quite large for a new settlement: slightly more than five miles (nine kilometers) long and two-thirds of a mile (one kilometer) wide. The streets of Amarna are especially wide, the houses are spacious and not crowded together, and there is not even a wall around the town, in keeping with Akhenaton's philosophy of brotherhood and peace.

Amarna was totally different from the other planned towns of Egypt. It was a bit like a resort town, because it was far from the crowds of the old capital. In the decorations of the palace buildings, a new type of art was used to ornament the new planned city. In the art of Amarna, the Pharaoh is portrayed not as a powerful and frightening figure, more god-like than human, but almost like an ordinary person. The paintings in the palace show the Pharaoh Akhenaton playing with his children, picking flowers, or resting by the side of a small pool in the palace courtyard. The people in these paintings are depicted with smiling faces, whereas in the past it has been extremely rare to see any trace of emotion in ancient Egyptian art.

Akhenaton died young, and his ambitious experiment died with him. Amarna was abandoned, the Egyptians returned once more to the old forms of worship, and one of the most ambitious and elegant planned cities of the ancient world fell into ruins.

The Land between Two Rivers

Far to the east of Greece and Egypt, in the heart of the Middle East, is the region of Mesopotamia, the land between the Tigris and Euphrates rivers. This area was the homeland of more than one great ancient civilization, and an important part of some of the great empires of the ancient world. The region of Mesopotamia was ruled by many different nations during its long history. Unlike Egypt, which was isolated by the Sahara Desert on either side, the people of Mesopotamia were never beyond the reach of hostile tribes or conquering armies.

In one respect, however, Egypt and Mesopotamia. had much in common. Both countries depended on the rivers that flowed through them to supply the water for irrigat-

The Pharaoh Akhenaton and his wife Nefertiti make offerings to the sun-god, Aton.

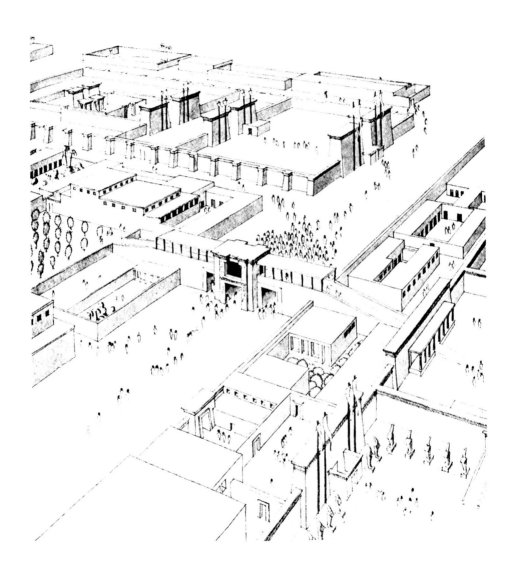

An artist's conception of one of the main streets in the city of Amarna

ing their crops. Mesopotamia, like Egypt, also developed a strong, centralized government hundreds and even thousands of years before the other people of the ancient world.

The architecture of Mesopotamia was greatly affected by the lack of building materials in the natural environment of the region. Mesopotamia had neither an adequate supply of stone nor an adequate supply of wood: therefore, the houses, palaces, fortresses, temples, and warehouses all had to be built of clay bricks. In an attempt to add at least a little variety to the uniformly dull color of the brick buildings, the Mesopotamians sometimes covered their walls with glazed bricks of various colors.

Although Mesopotamian civilization is incredibly old, the people of Mesopotamia practiced city planning quite early. The town of Shaddupum, which was built around 2000 B.C., is one of the early planned settlements of the region. Shaddupum was surrounded by a thick wall fortified by towers, and the two main streets of the town, wider than any of the other streets, divided the community into four quarters of equal size.

Some of the ancient clay tablets found in Mesopotamia contain descriptions of the founding of other planned cities. In one case, a Mesopotamian king tells of flattening a mound of ruins where the town of Calah once stood and rebuilding a new town on the ruins of the old.

Later rulers of Mesopotamia, the Assyrians, were fierce warriors who earned a reputation for cruelty among the people of the ancient world. Having secured a large empire by military conquest, the Assyrians were uneasy, fearing that some of their subjects might rise in revolt. For this reason, they moved entire populations from their original towns and villages and resettled them in new planned towns, which they built in different parts of their empire.

Earlier, we mentioned that some ancient rulers liked to build new capital cities for themselves when they came to power. You have already seen one example of that practice in the case of the Egyptian Pharaoh Akhenaton. The Assyrian king Sargon II also built a new capital – the city of Khorsabad – and he settled it with prisoners of war from many different lands. But two years after the new city was completed, Sargon II died, and his successor refused to live in the late king's capital. Taking the entire population

0 10 20 30

Above: The plan of Shaduppum, a Mesopotamian city built around 2000 B.C.

Right: This drawing pictures the Assyrian capital of Khorsabad, which was abandoned two years after it was completed.

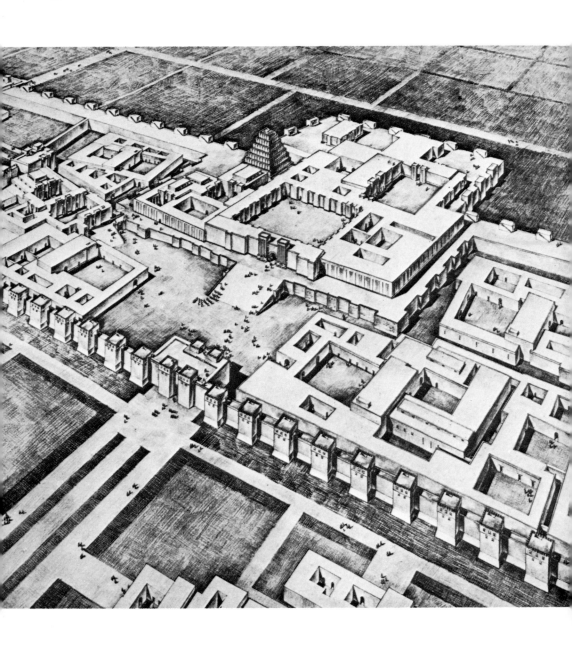

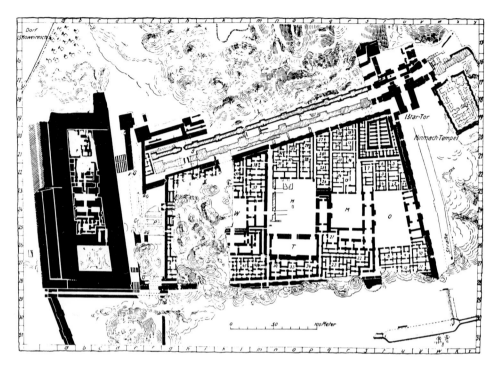

The plan of a section of Babylon, one of the largest and most impressive planned cities of the ancient world

with him, he moved to a town he ordered built for *himself,* and Khorsabad fell into ruins.

The last planned city of Mesopotamia we will mention is one you may already have heard of. It is called "Babylon." The Greek traveler Herodotus visited Babylon in the fifth century B.C., and he was greatly impressed. He told of a moat full of water running entirely around the city and of a city wall 80

feet (24 meters) wide and 300 feet (90 meters) high. It is difficult for us to imagine a wall of this size, because we simply do not build such structures in our society. Babylon's wall would have been wide enough to contain two single-family houses side by side within it; its height would have been equal to a 20- or 25-story building. Thieves and bandits would probably have some trouble climbing *that* wall in the night! There were, said Herodotus, 100 gates in the immense wall, and each gate was sealed with a door of brass. Within the city, houses three and four stories high lined a network of intersecting streets.

Conclusion

By now we have seen that city planning is indeed one of the oldest professional accomplishments of the human race. While the Greeks and Romans introduced the art of city planning to the western world, it had been practiced for thousands of years by much older civilizations. Like most of the other arts of civilization, city planning was not developed suddenly by a single person or even a single society. Instead, it evolved slowly, changing and improving as it was handed on from one society to another. No one can say for certain where it all began, but we do know that it did *not* begin with us.

GLOSSARY

aqueduct

A structure designed to carry water over long distances through a gradually sloping channel

acropolis

A fortress next to or inside of a Greek city, built on the highest ground

agora

A large area surrounded by columns, used in ancient Greece as the center of civic life

basilica

A Roman building used for assemblies and other public business

Capitolium

A Roman temple dedicated to Jupiter, Juno, and Minerva, always located on the highest ground of a Roman city

conquistadores

The early Spanish conquerors and colonizers of South and Middle America

forum

The main public square, marketplace, and civic center of a Roman city

hippodrome

An open-air stadium, used as a race track in ancient Greece and Rome

quarter	A section of a city, usually bordered by two or more main streets
sedan-chair	A covered chair supported on two poles and carried by two men, used as a conveyance
square	A large, open area inside a town or city, usually bordered by streets and surrounded on all sides by buildings
vault	An arched structure built of stone or brick, forming a ceiling or roof

INDEX

Pages listed in italics contain illustrations only.

ARTHUR SEGAL was born in Poland and emigrated to Israel in 1965. In that same year, he became a student of archaeology at the Hebrew University of Jerusalem. Mr. Segal's academic career was interrupted in 1970, when he was called to serve in the Israel Defence Force. After completing his military service, he continued his studies, concentrating his attention on the subject of town planning in the Middle East during the Hellenistic and the Roman periods. While attending the Hebrew University, Mr. Segal also participated in several archaeological excavations.

RICHARD L. CURRIER received his A.B. and Ph.D. degrees in anthropology from the University of California at Berkeley. He has done field work in Mexico and in Greece and has taught anthropology at Berkeley, at the University of Minnesota, and at the State University of New York in Plattsburgh. Dr. Currier now combines a teaching career with writing and research.